TEN BREATHS TO HAPPINESS

TEN BREATHS TO HAPPINESS
touching life in its fullness

GLEN SCHNEIDER
Foreword by Thich Nhat Hanh

PARALLAX
PRESS

Berkeley, California

Parallax Press
P.O. Box 7355
Berkeley, California 94707

Parallax Press is the publishing division of
Unified Buddhist Church, Inc.

Cover and text design by Elaine Chow
Cover and interior illustrations by Jason DeAntonis

Schneider, Glen, 1949-
 Ten breaths to happiness : touching life in its fullness /
Glen Schneider ; foreword by Thich Nhat Hanh.
     pages cm
 Summary: "Happiness is far more than a positive feeling that
comes and goes, happiness is wired into the physiology of
our brains. It is a skill we can all develop through cultivating
mindfulness and concentration. In Ten Breaths to Happiness
Schneider presents a series of simple practices and guided
meditations that allow you to literally rewire your neural pathways to experience deeper and more lasting fulfillment and
peace. Studies in neuroscience show that it takes about thirty
seconds to build a new neural-pathway. Schneider takes these
findings and combines them with mindfulness practices based
on the teachings of Zen teacher Thich Nhat Hanh. For example,
he encourages us to take ten conscious breaths whenever we
encounter something beautiful or have a meaningful experience. Consistently exercising this simple practice creates an
opportunity for the brain to move from its default reaction of
protection to one of appreciation and spaciousness."— Provided
by publisher.
 ISBN 978-1-937006-39-6 (pbk.)
1. Meditation—Zen Buddhism. 2. Spiritual life—Zen Buddhism.
I. Title.
 BQ9288.S36 2013
 294.3'4446--dc23
                                    2013008729

1 2 3 4 5 / 17 16 15 14 13

CONTENTS

FOREWORD

There are people who say that mindfulness is just one thing—breathing in and breathing out. They are right. With mindful breathing, we're more present for ourselves and for the world and we can live deeply every moment of our daily life. Mindful breathing helps us to be calm and happy and to have a clear mind. It helps us transform the suffering within. And it helps us to be in touch with the true nature of reality.

Mindful breathing takes a little training. But a few days of practice can already make a difference. We should be able to bring in a feeling of joy and happiness whenever we want to. We breathe in and bring our minds home to our bodies and suddenly we're fully present in the here and the now. It's very nourishing. And we're able to recognize the many conditions of happiness that are available—more than enough for us to be happy.

When you bring your mind home to your body, it's in order to be with your body, to be established in the here and the now, and to have a chance to live your life. You have an opportunity to live each moment deeply. You're no longer pulled away by thoughts about the past or the future, by your projects, or by strong emotions. Taking ten mindful breaths sounds simple, but the effect is enormous.

In your brain there are many well-travelled neural pathways. When you come into contact with something that habitually triggers a certain feeling in you, like the feeling of anger, your frequent travel along that neural pathway turns it into a habit—in this case, a habit of anger. With a mindful breathing practice, such as Ten Breaths, you can always open new neural pathways. And when that becomes a habit, we call it the habit of happiness. Any moment can be a moment of happiness.

We can all benefit from more happiness. So take time to breathe. This can make all the difference. You release, and you become a free person. As a free person, you see that there are many ways to respond to the same event, not just one way. When we're able to produce the energy of love and compassion, happiness is there. This is what we need most. This is what the world needs most.

—THICH NHAT HANH

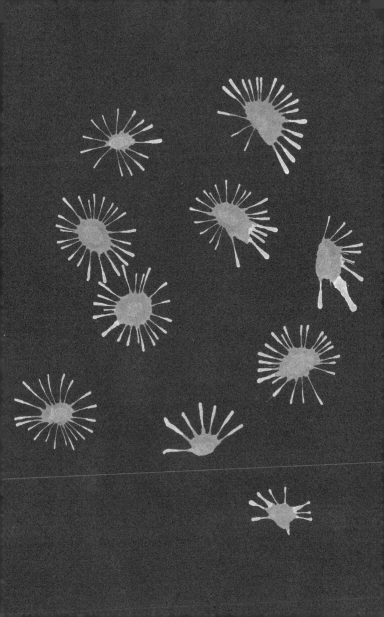

introduction
STOPPING TO SAVOR LIFE

Breathing in, I am aware that I am alive.
Breathing out, I smile to life within and around me.

—THICH NHAT HANH

The first time I tried the complete Ten Breaths practice, I was out in my garden on a crisp February evening. I was walking along a path when I looked up and saw the crescent moon framed by the bare branches of our buckeye tree. I stopped to take in this lovely scene, and while I was looking, I decided to take ten conscious breaths while looking at the moon in the branches. During those ten breaths, I noticed that somewhere in my chest I felt nourished in a way that was a little new. It was a small, pleasant feeling. Then I continued on my way.

The following night I went outside on an errand to the garage. I happened to look up and there was that crescent moon again, a little higher now, in the open sky. I stopped for just a moment—I don't know why—and as I did, I felt a rush of feeling, as if I were greeting a dear old friend, and these words bubbled up from deep inside: "Oh yeah, you and me, we go way back."

That surprised me, because I had never felt such a connection or had such a familiar feeling toward the moon. Then I remembered the link with my experience of the night before.

The Ten Breaths practice is a simple way to use conscious, rhythmic breathing to help us savor life and live more fully. It is quite simple. When something good and wonderful touches us—be it a sight, a sound, or a feeling—we stop and offer it our full presence for the length of ten breaths, so that we can really *taste* the experience of this present moment.

If we pay close attention, we can see that opportunities for happiness, for touching life's magnificence, actually present themselves many times each day. Something catches our eye; something touches our heart. Good feelings arise.

Gradually, I have trained myself to stop and experience more and more of these moments while breathing in and out ten times. Trees, birds, flowers, even my own body have all become good friends. I have rediscovered feelings of love and wonder that had been dormant in me since childhood. I have learned ways to deepen my connections with other people. My reverence for life has grown immeasurably, and so has my gratitude.

By happiness, I am speaking of the deep, abiding happiness of contentment, connection, and fulfillment, of dwelling happily in the present moment. This is the experience of opening to the goodness and wonders of life, enjoying life deeply, and feeling viscerally connected to others, the whole of creation, and the spiritual dimension.

Many people I talk with share a deep fear that they are somehow missing life; that they are alive but are not fully experiencing life. They feel they are only getting glimpses of life's promise. I know that feeling as well, and with me it has been deeply rooted.

Practicing Ten Breaths has shown me how to stop, open my heart, and savor what I love in the world— to let in the good. My life has blossomed in ways I would never have thought possible.

Overview of the Ten Breaths Practice

Here are the basic parts of the Ten Breaths practice. We'll go through them in more detail in Chapters Two, Three, and Four, in which you can learn the practice step by step.

When a beautiful moment presents itself and you encounter something that you would like to savor, such as sunlight on a dewdrop:

1   Stop whatever you are doing.

2   Close your eyes, put your dominant hand on your belly, and begin to pay attention to your breathing. Notice the rise and fall of your hand on your belly as you breathe. Take three deep breaths to settle and clear your mind.

3   When you feel more present, open your eyes and look at the object of your concentration. Take a deep slow breath in and out. That is "one."

4   Continue counting each breath: "two," "three," "four." Let your encounter unfold naturally. Just behold the object of your concentration and observe it without mental commentary or judgment as you count. Notice its color, shape, sound, or smell.

5   While counting, become aware of your body
    and any sensations or emotions that may arise.
    Allow every cell of your body to open up to the
    encounter. Allow the experience to be as full as
    possible. Don't hold back.

6   When you have reached "ten," rest in the feeling
    of the moment. Then, if you'd like, take ten more
    breaths in the same way.

The Ten Breaths practice is very simple in concept,
but can sometimes be challenging in practice. It takes
getting used to and requires focus and courage.
Often, it is hard simply to stop what we're doing and
make space to enjoy life more fully.

One way I learned to stop was by setting a goal of doing Ten Breaths at least once a day. At first, I chafed a
bit at this, but now it's second nature. I look forward
to each day's new encounter. It's so much fun. What
will call me, what will touch my heart, what will be
my treat for the day?

Last week, I was walking along a creek bank and I noticed a spring-green cluster of California bee plant stems sprouting up at the base of a valley oak. As I walked by, I heard myself saying, "That is so beautiful!" Then a little voice inside said, "This is a Ten Breath moment." So I backed up in my tracks and gave the moment Ten Breaths. My eyes feasted on the rich, shiny purple of the new stems, the slanting sunlight catching the leaves, their zigzag margins, and how they trembled in the puff of a breeze. These were all things I'd never noticed about this plant before, and it was thrilling to discover so much new and beautiful in the world. I felt like the richest person on Earth, and I was having such a great time that I actually gave the scene Ten Breaths three or four times over.

The important thing in practicing Ten Breaths is to get started and set your intention to keep on counting with your breath all the way to "ten." When you do this, you create new neural pathways that help anchor your habit of happiness.

The Ten Breaths practice engages the teacher within. What catches your attention is entirely, uniquely up to you. How you behold your experience and how it unfolds is completely yours. You can practice this anywhere, anytime. When something speaks to you, give it your full respect and the time it deserves. You will be richly rewarded.

Our hands imbibe like roots,
so I place them on what is
beautiful in this world.

—FRANCIS OF ASSISI

chapter one

NEW PATHWAYS TO HAPPINESS

The Ten Breaths practice is a kind of training. When we train the body, we exercise to help our muscles grow and develop. The mind is similar; with practice we can help it learn the habits of happiness and nourish our deepest aspirations.

We can learn to approach life in the spirit of Francis of Assisi. He understood that we "imbibe" the world. He practiced touching "what is beautiful in this world." He spoke of using his hands. We can use our entire presence to connect with what is beautiful, wholesome, and nourishing.

This approach to life has been underscored by three recent discoveries in neuroscience:

1   Our brains are comprised of cells called neurons, which connect together chemically and electrically in clusters called neural pathways. Our sense impressions, memories, abilities, and emotional patterns are all encoded this way in the physiology of the brain. Mental traffic tends to follow existing routes, regardless of whether the neural pathway is appropriate, accurate, or actually beneficial. Beginning in childhood, the more we repeat a pattern, the more habitual it becomes. As psychologist Rick Hanson writes, "What happens in your mind changes your brain, both temporarily and in lasting ways; neurons that fire together wire together."[*]

* See Rick Hanson and Richard Mendius, *Buddha's Brain: The Practical Neuroscience of Happiness, Love, and Wisdom* (Oakland, CA: New Harbinger Publications, Inc., 2009).

2   The human organism is preferentially wired—
overwhelmingly—to recognize danger and
threats. Survival is paramount. Happiness and joy
are secondary behaviors, but they can be learned.

3   Neuroscientists have found that it takes about
thirty seconds of stimulation to firmly root a new
neural pathway. A new neural pathway becomes
more firmly rooted the longer an experience
is held in awareness and the more intense the
emotional stimulation. As new connections are
created and used repeatedly, footpaths eventually
become freeways. With practice we can rewire
our brains so that patterns of happiness become
habitual and deeply nourishing.

The Ten Breaths practice incorporates these findings
of neuroscience in a practical way. Meditation traditions have long used the practice of counting the
breath to ten as a way of sustaining concentration. It
also happens that it takes a minute or more to take

ten conscious breaths. So if we combine counting ten breaths with our positive experiences, we have a generous measure of the time needed to firmly root and strengthen a new pathway.

Establishing new patterns of happiness and rooting them physiologically requires that we do these two things, which are the heart of the Ten Breath practice:

- Sustain positive experiences for at least thirty seconds.

- Feel positive experiences *in the body* as fully as possible.

We use the breath to stop our thinking and connect our minds and bodies. The breath can become the doorway to an awareness of our bodily sensations, emotions, and our memories. Best of all, since we always have our breath with us, we can do this practice anytime, anywhere.

I used to think that happiness was like good weather—here sometimes, not here at other times. Happiness would come and go, and it was definitely not in my control. After my experience with the moon and the buckeye tree, I saw a different possibility. I could actively use the Ten Breaths practice to nourish what was good and beautiful in myself, and to gradually change my relationship with the world. With this practice, I learned that I could *choose* happiness and water the seeds of it with my breath.

We are not able to choose everything that happens to us and we will, no matter what we do, experience difficulties. But, increasing our happiness is definitely within our power. This is revolutionary.

The greatest of all miracles

is to be alive,

and when you breathe in,

you touch that miracle.

—THICH NHAT HANH

chapter two

COUNTING TEN BREATHS

Ten Breaths is a "whole organism" practice in which we bring our bodies and minds together in a focused way, so we can be really present for life. Often, our thinking minds are in one place and our bodies are somewhere else. For example, if your partner brings you a bouquet of flowers and, as you take them into your hands, you are actually thinking about something that happened earlier at work, you are not fully present for the experience and not able to enjoy it fully. Body and mind are disconnected.

In meditation practice, a time-tested way to bring body and mind back together is by focusing our minds on our breathing. Breathing is the flowing energy of the body in motion. If we can focus our mind's attention on the simple reality of breathing in and breathing out for a period of time, the body and mind become connected, and we naturally calm down and feel more present.

The Ten Breaths practice focuses on breath as the bridge that connects body and mind. When helping others learn the Ten Breaths practice, I've found it helpful to break the process into two components: counting with the body and centering in the body. We'll learn and practice these two components separately at first, and then combine them. In this chapter, we'll focus on counting; in the next chapter, we'll focus on centering; and then we'll practice combining them.

Counting Ten Breaths with the Body

Counting to ten is an established meditation practice for developing focus and concentration. In the Ten Breaths practice, the purpose of counting to ten is to keep our attention focused on our chosen object of concentration long enough to establish and deepen a neural pathway. In this way, the next time we see this object, our happiness is more accessible and comes more quickly.

One way to practice counting ten breaths is with our fingers. This allows the body to do the counting and frees the mind from the need to say the numbers and keep track. The body can actually learn to count quite quickly.

LET'S TRY THIS NOW:

1   Sit down and place your dominant hand on your belly with your fingers comfortably

spread. (Your hand may rest either on your clothing or on your skin.)

2 To relax and clear your mind, close your eyes and take three deep breaths. A "breath" is one in-breath and one out-breath. Notice the movement of your belly and the rise and fall of your hand.

3 When your breathing has become calm and relaxed, start counting your breaths. With the first in-breath, gently press and release your thumb on your belly to mark "one." Keep your attention on your breathing, and when the next in-breath begins, gently press and release your forefinger on your belly to mark "two." Continue counting on the rest of your fingers until you reach "five."

4   To count six, go back to your thumb again
    and continue counting through all your
    fingers again until you reach "ten." If your
    attention wanders, start over again with
    "one." Eventually, you will get to the point
    where the counting is just a tiny happening
    in the background of your awareness.

The reason why we learn to count on one hand is so
we can hold an object that we would like to encounter
in the other hand, while counting without interrup-
tion. The point is to be fully present and to count
with your body for the length of time it takes to
breathe ten times.

If you are in a public place and you want to count ten
breaths, you might feel self-conscious putting your
hand on your belly. In that case, or if it's just more
comfortable for you, you may want to gently put one
hand on top of the other and count that way, or count

with your fingers on your thigh. You can press your fingers against your other hand, or against your thigh, just the same as you would against your belly.

Last fall a group of us gathered for a day of meditation during which I was teaching Ten Breaths. We began indoors, where we practiced counting Ten Breaths with the fingers of one hand lightly touching our bodies. For the next step, we took the noncounting hand itself as the focus of another Ten Breaths; we each counted to ten using the fingers of one hand, as we encountered the presence of the other hand. Finally, we took Ten Breaths outdoors to see what delights we might encounter. One woman was drawn to a specially colored leaf of a tree. With Ten Breaths, she examined the veins of the leaf, and they reminded her of the lines in the palm of her hand. She saw that the leaves of the tree and the hands of her body were actually very similar, and the tree suddenly became for her this marvelous creature with all these wondrous, waving hands.

Abandoning myself
to breathing out
and letting breathing in
naturally fill me.

—KEIZAN ZENJI,
FOURTEENTH CENTURY JAPAN

chapter three

CENTERING IN THE BODY

In this chapter, we will focus on the sensations of breathing out. In my experience, the out-breath is accompanied by very pleasant sensations in the body, connected with relaxing and releasing tension. When this happens, we can have a feeling of being "centered," of being fully present in our bodies. Athletes and performers center themselves in preparation for an event. We can center ourselves in our bodies in preparation for meeting life.

Breathing out, we may notice a gentle whooshing feeling in our abdomens of letting go of tension. I experience this as a wave of relaxation that moves from my chest to my belly. Sometimes I imagine myself at the top of a slide, with a chest full of air. As the out-breath begins its release, I glide down the slide as if nothing else exists in the world.

We cultivate "abandoning ourselves to breathing out" in the same spirit that we may abandon ourselves—or yield completely—to joy. When the out-breath is completely released, there may be a delightful space of calm before the next in-breath begins to fill us.

LET'S TRY THIS NOW:

1 Sit down, close your eyes, and take three deep breaths to help you relax and clear your mind.

2 Simply notice your normal, relaxed in-breath filling you naturally. Completely relax your mind

and body as you let your out-breath flow out in a relaxed way.

3 Do this several times, "abandoning" yourself to breathing out, completely letting yourself relax into the sensations of your out-flowing breath.

4 Continue breathing in this way. As you breathe out, bring your awareness to your abdomen and see if you feel sensations of relaxing and calming as you let go of your out-breath.

5 With each out-breath, let yourself sink deeper and deeper into this relaxing sensation in your body. Settle deeper and deeper into your body.

When we let ourselves breathe in this manner, right away we become more relaxed and open, more present in our bodies. A dear friend of mine particularly loves this "abandoning myself to breathing out" practice because each out-breath clears the mind, over and over again.

Last autumn, he and I were out on our favorite hike in Castle Rock Park, near California's Mount Diablo. The sandstone cliffs there rise up several hundred feet to form turret-shaped mountains against the sky. We like to go there in the late afternoon, have a picnic dinner on the trail, and walk back in the darkness listening to the crickets. This time, a full moon rose above the mountains as we walked on the road without flashlights, just in the moonlight. As we rounded a bend, the oak forest formed a bower over the road, etching it with moon shadows. My friend stopped and said with a smile, "Is this a Ten Breath moment?"

Of course it was. We stopped and breathed in silence, abandoning ourselves to moonlight, shadows, and friendship.

Focus on your emotions and body sensations, since these are the essence of implicit memory. Let the experience fill your body and be as intense as possible.

—RICK HANSON

chapter four

COMBINING COUNTING AND CENTERING

Now, we are ready to combine the elements of counting ten breaths and centering and relaxing ourselves. When we combine them, it creates a new synergy that is much greater than the sum of the parts. When the practice works, it can help remove the unconscious barriers that often separate us from other people and the rest of the world, and that get in the way of being fully present to enjoy life.

Learning to combine the counting and centering of the Ten Breaths practice may feel awkward at first. I remember how as a child I struggled to learn how to ride a bicycle. There was the pedaling, the steering, and the braking, and I just couldn't learn to put them all together. My method of stopping was to ride directly into the mailbox, grab hold of it, and let the bike tumble over. Finally, with practice, it clicked for me (and I'm sure the mailbox appreciated that too). Learning Ten Breaths is a little tricky like that. If you have difficulty at first, you may like to practice it several times a day at home, sitting with your eyes closed. Then it will begin to feel more natural.

LET'S TRY THIS NOW:

1 Sit down, close your eyes, and place your hand on your abdomen, as you've done before.

2 Take three deep breaths to settle and clear your mind.

3   Then start counting. Press and release your thumb on your belly to mark your first inhale, and as you breathe out become aware of any sense of relaxation in your body.

4   Continue breathing and counting, marking each breath with your fingers and focusing on the relaxing sensations of breathing out. With each out-breath, let yourself relax and open more deeply.

5   Continue counting with your fingers and abandoning yourself to breathing out until you have completed ten breaths.

After I had practiced Ten Breaths for a couple of weeks I was able to naturally combine both elements while at the same time focusing on something that caught my attention in the world. This way of being has now become my basis for encountering the world.

One day recently, I was walking home from downtown Berkeley after treating myself to a praline pecan ice-cream cone. The sun was shining and the world seemed mighty good. Passing in front of the high school, I looked down to the corner and noticed the big redwood tree in front of City Hall. This tree is the largest—and tallest—tree in town.

I decided to give the moment Ten Breaths. I moved to the edge of the sidewalk. Standing still, I closed my eyes and took a few breaths. Then I opened my eyes, put my right hand on my belly, and began to count with my fingertips.

By the third or fourth breath, I was feeling waves of relaxation moving from my chest to my belly. I continued counting. On the eighth breath a glowing feeling arose in my chest and spread to my face as a huge smile blossomed. I felt a barrier in myself dissolve and the tree became alive. I whispered, "Oh, you magnificent creature." Yes, there she was, the grand matriarch, in all her glory, all 152 feet of her. There she was, so tall and fine in the warm October sun, her many arms outspread with each end tipped up toward the sky.

I walked down the street with a skip in my step, and my heart was flying high.

One learns that the world,

though made, is yet being made;

that this is still

the morning of creation.

—JOHN MUIR

chapter five

TOUCHING THE WONDERS OF LIFE

We have learned the basics of the Ten Breaths practice. Now we can move out into the world and use it to touch life's wonders.

In the classical world, people spoke of four elements that make up all of creation: air, earth, fire, and water. So before setting you loose to touch what calls you in this world, please make a date with me. I want to show you something amazing. We can use Ten Breaths in the encounter. It will take only a few minutes.

Come on outside. Let's find some sunshine. We are going to encounter fire.

When you have found some sunshine, sit down, relax, and close your eyes. Tilt your head so your face can catch the sun. Feel its warmth on your face and hands. (If the sun is still too bright through your closed eyes, you can shade them with your hand.) Hold that position with your eyes closed and now meet the sun with Ten Breaths:

- Place your hand on your belly and center yourself

- Take a breath and start counting with "one"

- Relax into your body as you breathe out

- Continue counting to ten, with full awareness of your feelings and body sensations

Now, open your eyes. Look at your hands, look at the life around you, look at the sunshine. That light, that heat, that fire is the energy of the sun. It fuels life on Earth. It is the energy that powers your counting, your breathing, your thinking, and your projects. It is the energy of all the people you hold most dear.

The plants catch the sun's energy and combine it with air, water, and earth to make their branches, leaves, fruits, and roots. The fiber of plant bodies is the food base that sustains you and me and nearly all life on Earth. Now draw a line from the sun through the plants to your body: this is the essential circuit that powers your life. We are all creatures of the sun. It is our second heart beating in the sky.

Now it is time to move out into the world. When something touches your heart, stop and meet it with Ten Breaths. Ten Breaths is a concentration practice for stopping to savor the good in life. Please don't limit yourself. Use it for whatever calls you: petting your dog, eating chocolate, enjoying a sunset, feelings of friendship, flowers, trees, and the stars. When something wonderful calls you, let the happiness suffuse your entire being.

Time flies like an arrow;

if we do not live deeply,

we waste our lives.

—GUISHAN LINGYOU,
NINTH CENTURY CHINA

chapter six

DEEPENING OUR HUMAN CONNECTIONS

The Ten Breaths practice can be used to encounter and deepen our good feelings about other people. This can enhance our relationships and make them more harmonious. Instead of placing our attention on "what is beautiful in this world," we place our attention on the wholesome emotions that arise in us when we're in connection with other people.

We use exactly the same technique of stopping, counting, breathing, and opening. You can take advantage of any moment when you're feeling good about some-one. Just stop and give Ten Breaths to the feeling.

If someone offers you a kindness, you can stop and give it Ten Breaths. If you are thinking about another person and a loving feeling comes up, you can give that Ten Breaths, too. Or, if you are with someone you feel close to and they know the practice, you can do Ten Breaths together. You may have to be creative to find a subtle way to stop and practice Ten Breaths when you're in the presence of other people. The flow of human interaction tends to move forward very quickly. It is often difficult to press the pause button.

Not long ago, I got a caring email from a dear friend in response to a personal trouble I had shared with her. Reading her email, I felt very loved and under-stood. I noticed how wonderful it felt to be cared about. I also noticed that I had another twenty-five emails waiting in my inbox for responses.

Before opening the next email, I decided to stop and practice Ten Breaths to really take in the good feeling I had from reading my friend's note. Sitting there in front of the monitor, I just closed my eyes, put my hand on my belly, and started breathing, greeting this feeling within me. I noticed the feeling getting stronger, and then mellowing. As I breathed, a little voice inside me whispered, "Yes, this is good, you really do have this feeling. It is wonderful. You really are loved and you do feel just this good." It was wonderful to bask in the glow, and in the afterglow, of such a feeling. Then I opened my eyes and got back to responding to mail.

Another time, I was talking with a friend on the phone. She was overflowing with a wonderful story of family reconciliation. Her mother and her family had been estranged from her mom's sister for a long time. Her mom had not spoken to my friend's aunt for fifty years. After all these years, my friend had finally gotten up the courage to reach out to her aunt, and so they had agreed to meet at a restaurant.

My friend and her brother had lived in an orphanage as children because their mother was mentally ill and their father was in prison. In the conversation at the restaurant, the true story unfolded. Her aunt revealed that at the time, although she'd been asked and had wanted to, she'd felt unable to take care of her niece and nephew so that they wouldn't have to live in the orphanage. The aunt had struggled deeply with this request, but in the end she'd been unable to say yes. She had her own dreams. The aunt felt guilty about letting the family down. She'd avoided the family all these years because of her great shame. As her story tumbled out, many tears were shed. They hugged and rediscovered their love. The family was healing.

In telling me this story, my friend was still full of emotion. I was as well. Even though we were on the phone, I said, "Let's honor this moment with Ten

Breaths." And so we did, each of us practicing Ten Breaths, and letting the feelings sink in. We were nurturing the neural pathways of new happiness.

Another time, my wife and I were eating dinner. We've been married for over forty years. Our children are grown now, so it's just the two of us most of the time. We were sitting at the table; the food was tasty; the conversation was companionable; and I was feeling very warm and homey. I realized how much I appreciated her. I didn't say anything. I didn't close my eyes or move my hand to my belly. I just started taking Ten Breaths, looking at her and seeing her goodness as she ate. On about the fifth breath, she looked up and asked, "Is something wrong? You got so quiet."

"No," I responded, "I was just appreciating you. I was doing Ten Breaths." She put her fork down. I could see she was touched. Leaning back in her chair, she said with a glow, "Oh, that's so nice."

Those who feel cut off have to learn how to practice so that they will feel connected again with the source of life that has brought them there. That by itself can help bring them into the heart of life and remove all kinds of fear.

—THICH NHAT HANH

chapter seven

TOUCHING THE EARTH AND
OUR SOURCES OF LIFE

At its core, Ten Breaths is essentially a concentration practice that you can apply to almost any practice or situation. You can even use it to encounter deeply good moments that have just passed, or moments from long ago.

One of my very favorite Plum Village practices is Three Touchings of the Earth.* This is a practice for connecting with our ancestors and our descendants, the Earth

* See Thich Nhat Hanh, *Teachings on Love* (Berkeley, CA: Parallax Press, 2007), Chapter 14.

and all beings, and the many sources of life that have made our life possible and that sustain us. We can stop and bring our full awareness to our ancestors. We can bring this awareness to all species that are present in this world with us. When we are deeply aware of our many connections, we can remove many fears, including the fear of death.

In describing how we often feel alone and isolated, Thich Nhat Hanh uses the image of a flower:

> We are all flowers, and we may wither several times a week, or each day, just because we do not take care of ourselves. If you pick a flower and leave it on the table for a few hours you will see that the flower will not be able to continue as a flower, because it has been disconnected from the tree, the earth, the source of life. This may be described as the phenomenon of alienation.

In Three Touchings of the Earth, we connect with our ancestors and descendants, with all beings, and with the universe. It is usually done lying face-down on the earth or the floor, but it can be done in any body position or situation. We consider three contemplations:

1 I connect with all ancestors and descendants of my blood, spiritual, and land families.

2 I connect with all people and all species, who are present at this moment in this world with me.

3 I let go of my idea that I am this body and that my lifespan is limited.

When we do this practice in a group, someone reads a section of text as we lie facedown (or "crouch like an egg") on the earth or floor, with our head, forearms, and shins all touching the earth or floor. We allow any images or feelings that arise to flow through us naturally. We can also use the Ten Breaths practice to choose one image and deepen our connections with it.

This can be very nourishing and healing.

Recently, we practiced this in our local meditation community (or Sangha) that gathers weekly. First, we closed our eyes and warmed up with a round of Ten Breaths for our counting and then a second round for our centering. Then, as the first Earth-touching—for getting in touch with ancestors and descendants— was read, each of us focused in our own minds on a memory of an ancestor or a descendant. When a strong image arose, we used Ten Breaths to encounter it more fully.

Afterward, we went around the circle to share our experiences. One person had brought to mind a special time when his mother had said she loved him. He shared how the Ten Breaths had helped him feel more secure in his mother's love. Another person reported enormous gratitude in reconnecting with a grandfather she hadn't thought of in over twenty years.

Another woman described reconnecting with a beloved cat who had died several years before. She recounted how when the image of her cat came up, she felt a lot of grief, and she realized that she had not fully processed her feelings about her cat's death. She was grateful for the opportunity to reconnect. She shared that what she most loved about her cat was the feeling that she could be completely herself around the cat, and "what a gift that was." She went on to say, "Maybe someday I'll be able to be completely myself around my brother and the rest of my family. I'm not there yet, but reconnecting with my cat has given me hope that there could be a way, and for that I'm very grateful."

Another time when we all met, we practiced the Second Earth-touching—connecting with all species alive with us in this moment. As our focus, we each held a buckeye seed in one hand. A California buckeye seed is the size of a tangerine, and one fills your hand nicely. They are really gorgeous: chestnut-brown, smooth and shiny, lavishly marbled with color. That evening, we encountered our buckeye seeds with three rounds of Ten Breaths, going deeper each time.

In our sharing afterward, one person noted happily, but with a little embarrassment, that she had begun to experience feelings of affection toward her buckeye seed. Several people nodded in agreement. We continued our sharing around the circle until it came to another woman, who just happened to be there with her partner. As this woman spoke, she became more animated. "I don't just love my buckeye," she said with a devilish twinkle, "I want to marry it!"

*Still, in a way, we do not
see a flower, really.
It is so small. We haven't time.
To see takes time,
as to have a friend takes time.*

—GEORGIA O'KEEFE

chapter eight

WHEN OBSTACLES ARISE

I believe we are all the same in wanting to be happy. But as we begin to touch our happiness more authentically, we may also awaken past disappointments and difficulties with finding happiness. Our deeper feelings, both positive and negative, tend to be mingled together, and activating one feeling can activate others. These obstacles are part of us, too, encoded in our neural networks, and it is natural that they will arise.

So it may take some courage to actually *pursue* happiness. In my experience, if we want to be happier and live more deeply, we will have to learn how to deal with our obstacles.

I have found three effective strategies for dealing with obstacles to happiness:

1 Nourishing our happiness through regular practice

2 Recognizing our deep-seated obstacles and their roots

3 Removing our obstacles by embracing their energy

Nourishing Our Happiness
through Regular Practice

Repetition is the key to forming new habits. By doing the Ten Breaths practice again and again, you will strengthen and deepen new neural pathways. With each success, your confidence will grow and the practice will feel more natural.

In my tradition of Plum Village Buddhism, named after the French monastery founded by Zen Master Thich Nhat Hanh, twenty-one days is used as a measure of time long enough to form a new habit. I would suggest that you set a goal of doing Ten Breaths at least once a day for twenty-one days. This goal can motivate you. You may want to schedule a few minutes each day to stop and practice for Ten Breaths. It may be helpful to keep a written log. Write down the date and the focus of each new Ten Breaths experience, along with any obstacles you encounter.

When I first started doing the Ten Breaths practice, I would many times feel a wave of anxiety envelop me at breath three or four. I would feel a scary, agitated pressure in my heart and lung area. By breath six I would sometimes find myself crying for a breath or two. I found that if I just kept counting, I would arrive at ten feeling wonderful. That was an important lesson about persevering. Gradually, those fireworks went away and have not resurfaced.

We have a lot of inertia to overcome, and we are naturally wired to be cautious about change. The psychotherapist Harville Hendrix writes, "The only way to lessen this automatic resistance is to repeat a new behavior often enough so that it begins to feel familiar and therefore safe."*

One way to help us feel safe in our own bodies is to first practice Deep Relaxation. This involves scanning the body lovingly to release tension and is a very

---

* Harville Hendrix, *Getting the Love You Want*, rev.ed. (New York, NY: Henry Holt & Co., 1st ed. 1998, rev. ed. 2001).

effective way to bring calm and peace to the body and mind. Deep Relaxation is described in detail in Appendix 1.

Another way to support your practice of happiness is through a group. When joining a meditation community, you can benefit from the collective energy of practice, share experiences, and support each other.

Remember, we are rewiring ourselves. It takes time. Diligence is a virtue and change will not happen all at once. Keep practicing, even if it causes anxiety at first. Consider doing Ten Breaths until it becomes a beautiful habit.

Recognizing Our Deeper Obstacles
and Their Roots

Obstacles to happiness come in many forms. With practice, we can learn to recognize them and the real events of our lives that lie at their roots.

One of my earliest memories is of being downtown in Walnut Creek, California, where I grew up. I was about four and it had rained that morning. I was standing on the sidewalk holding my mother's hand when I noticed with delight the reflection of the trees and buildings upside-down in the puddles. In my joy, I exclaimed, "Mommy, they're upside-down, look!"

She responded by pulling my arm and saying, "Oh, come along. We don't have time for that kind of foolishness." I remember her tone was very angry, and that it scared me. It must have made a huge impression because for much of my life, I have carried this deep fear that joyous delight is "foolishness," and we don't have time for it. This has been one of *my* obstacles.

Here are some common obstacles to happiness that I have observed in others and myself:

* *We may have difficulty stopping.* Our daily lives are so busy; it can be hard to stop.

- *We may need someone else with us to share the moment.* We believe the presence of another person can help us to open up space for our feelings and validate them.

- *We may feel a little numb.* We may have a hard time connecting with our feelings.

- *We may feel undeserving, or even guilty.* How can we be happy when there's so much suffering in the world, or when we feel we may have caused pain to others?

- *We may feel overwhelmed by big feelings.* Strong feelings of happiness may be frightening and make us feel out of control.

- *We may believe that being happy can be dangerous.* We may have been shamed or punished for being happy. We may feel that if we relax our vigilance and enjoy ourselves, bad things could happen.

These obstacles and these feelings are all real. They are the energy of our old neural pathways—habits and messages formed in real life. There are very good reasons for their power. And at their root, they are based in fear. They are trying to protect us from harm. But they often overdo it. As we learn to recognize our obstacles more clearly and understand their roots, they begin to lose their power.

Our desire to be happy is also powerful. If we can develop this energy by having successes in the practice, we build a stronger base from which to address our fears. Taking the longer view, we may notice a continual back-and-forth as we grow in our capacity to live more happily and to meet our obstacles. Gradually, our capacity for happiness will increase.

A lot is at stake in learning to get past our fear. Harville Hendrix explains it this way: "When it comes to our own repressed emotions, we cower in fear. We fear that what is inside of us is dark, ugly, and overpowering. But once we gain the courage to wrestle with this fear, we learn an astonishing fact: what is hiding inside us is our own blocked life energy. It is love; it is light; it is the essence of God."*

* Ibid.

Most of my clients who terminate therapy prematurely do so not because they are unable to make positive changes, but because they can't cope with the anxiety that the positive changes bring about.

—HARVILLE HENDRIX

chapter nine

REMOVING OUR OBSTACLES

Some obstacles to happiness may prove to be deep-seated and very resistant. In this case, we can use the Ten Breaths practice to help transform them directly. We drop beneath the thinking mind and touch the truth of the body.

As our experience of happiness deepens, anxieties and fears may surface. Change can bring up anxiety. This anxiety has its roots in the fact that we're going against our established patterns. The organism becomes nervous and deep down it fears consequences, perhaps even death.

I have found that pursuing happiness single-mindedly with Ten Breaths will inevitably bring us face to face with some of our deeper sufferings. But grounded in real happiness, we will have the stability—and practice tools—needed to transform these feelings and be free from them. It is indeed a great happiness to be free from suffering.

We often project obstacles on to people or situations. We create stories about them. To get to the roots of our obstacles, we need to go inward, connecting with our body feelings and sensations. When these obstacles are bathed at the source in the energy of our breathing, they begin to release their tension and, with it, their power. This process can be called Removing the Object.* It is very healing.

---

* The Removing the Object practice is also very effective for transforming deep suffering and trauma. This is a practice adapted from the teachings of ninth-century Chinese Zen Master Linji. See Appendix 2 for a more detailed presentation.

LET'S TRY THIS NOW:

1   Sit down, close your eyes, and place your hand on your belly.

2   Take several deep breaths to settle and clear your mind.

3   Call to mind a charged issue, person, or situation. This is the object. Now begin counting and relaxing into your body sensations.

4   As you continue breathing and counting, let go of any thinking about the object. Completely open yourself to the feelings and sensations in your body, especially the areas of greatest energy, tension, or charge.

5   As you breathe in, imagine sending your breath to these areas of tension, and as you breathe out, release the tension in your body and your feelings.

6   Continue this process of releasing tension. You may need to do several cycles of Ten Breaths. Continue this until you feel more peaceful.

We are seldom upset for the reason we think we are. I remember once longing to see a certain friend who had unexpectedly and painfully cut off all contact with me years before. I was home alone, sitting on the couch upstairs; it was hot and stuffy, and I don't know why, but I imagined how wonderful it would be if we could sit together by a babbling creek and just share all the delights of nature we would be seeing there. But, this wasn't possible right now, and I began to despair. I couldn't seem to shake this unpleasant feeling and so I decided to try the practice of Removing the Object.

I closed my eyes, put my hand on my belly, and starting relaxing into my breathing. I began to surrender to my body sensations. Soon my body started to shake, and I was flooded with fear. "No," I said to myself. "I can't do this. It's too hard and too scary." I had a sharp, desperate feeling that I was still unable to connect with some core, bedrock aspiration in myself, that I was still missing some vitally central feature of life. For several minutes I just sat and breathed. I noticed I was trembling and I didn't try and stop it. I had learned, from previous meditation practice, that these old emotions lie deep in the body and it can be very beneficial when we let the body release the energy it's been holding.

Gradually, the storm inside me began to die down. I became more peaceful. Then another energy began to arise, and I became suffused with a tremendous desire to go out into nature and put my hands on the rocks and the trees and to feel the very pulse of life. I asked myself, "What could I do, right in that very moment?" I looked at my hand, and looking closely, I could see that my hand was part of nature, too. Nature was right here. The ridges of my fingerprints were as much a part of nature as the furrowed bark of an oak tree. "I *am* nature," I realized. "I don't have to go anywhere." All thoughts of my lost friend had completely vanished—the object had been removed. Looking deeply, I can see I was encountering seeds of my oldest fears, sown by my mother's reproaches. We are seldom upset for the reason we think we are.

You might occasionally be surprised at the strong emotions that can arise when you do this practice. But staying with the body feelings lets the difficulties release and ease.

Sometimes, our feelings can seem overwhelming. When this happens, we can use a technique called Touch and Rest. First, we touch the energy in the body for Ten Breaths; then we rest by opening our eyes and placing our attention on something pleasant out in the world for a while. When we feel more stable, we can close our eyes and go inside again and touch the body energy with Ten Breaths again. We can touch and rest, back and forth, and let the energy gradually transform.

Several months after the experience of discovering that my hand was part of nature, I was on a retreat at a small meditation center. We had been doing several rounds of Ten Breaths practice in the meditation hall, first with the counting, then with the centering. Since it was a beautiful spring day and we were in the countryside, we were asked to go outdoors to discover whatever would call us. Then we would stop and give it Ten Breaths.

I was drawn to sit on a rock outcropping overlooking the creek. There I found trees, birds, water, sunshine, and fresh air. As I practiced breathing in and out, these words arose:

> Reflections calling, trees upside-down again;
> Sky between the branches, floating on the water.
> Now it's all wiggling, now a lazuli bunting;
> Hi Mom—doing great!

You only have to let
the soft animal of your body
love what it loves.

—MARY OLIVER

chapter ten

THE HABIT OF HAPPINESS

If you have gotten this far, I hope you have already stopped along the way and had many successes with this practice. I hope you have been able to connect more deeply with your happiness and the wonders of life. I hope you have been opening up and strengthening new neural pathways.

Whatever your experience with the Ten Breaths practice, it may be helpful to remember that the heart of the practice—establishing new patterns of happiness and rooting them physiologically—rests in these two essentials:

- Sustain positive experiences for at least thirty seconds.

- Feel positive experiences *in the body* as fully as possible.

Let us now consider the cumulative effect of many positive encounters. In a short period of time, the effect is very good. In a longer period of time, the effect can be profound. Happiness can become a habit, the dominant mode of your life, and not just an occasional delight. A fundamental shift is possible.

I grew up in a dysfunctional, alcoholic family. I was the victim of various forms of physical and mental abuse and violence. There was no one to protect me. Loving what I loved—be it family, friends, camping, flowers, seedpods, or even reflections in a puddle—felt dangerous and even life-threatening. The natural love in my body shriveled like a raisin and left a large hole.

On my own spiritual path, I have encountered many difficulties, especially my fear. It has taken many years to relearn how to touch my feelings more deeply. I kept going because I could see that I was becoming happier. I could feel my goodness more clearly. I was touching life more authentically, and that gave me strength to keep opening and to keep honoring my love. At some point, I noticed that a profound shift had taken place in me.

If we pay close attention, we can see that opportunities for happiness present themselves many times, perhaps hundreds of times, each day. We discover that "soft animal body" inside of ourselves. We can learn to recognize the voice of that visceral part of ourselves that continually notices what it loves. This soft animal body forever beckons us to embrace and savor this world. The question is not about whether there are opportunities; the question is how we respond to these opportunities.

How do we learn to make loving what we love a habit? What will happen if we are successful?

Your intention to be happy is fundamental. If you can resolve to use the Ten Breaths practice to encounter something positive at least once a day for twenty-one days, you will be on the right track. New, healthy neural pathways will develop and strengthen, and the practice will get easier and feel more natural. Along with your increasing happiness, obstacles will arise, and they will also need to be addressed.

You may gradually discover that you have entered a new paradigm: that it has become second nature to "place your hands on what is beautiful in this world." The flow of your life will move from happiness to happiness, and you will find that you begin to naturally expect this. The difficulties will not all disappear, but they will become mere bumps in the road. You will learn to trust your love and be eager to encounter the world and its many wonders.

If you keep doing this practice, you will notice that as you feel more connected, you will also feel less fear. The fear of dying will lessen, because one of the strongest roots of that fear is the fear of missing life, of missing this precious, amazing experience.

Once you begin to touch your happiness and the wonders of life habitually, the world naturally begins to look different. You will viscerally feel and know that you are part of the stream of life. You will discover limitless opportunities to encounter beauty and goodness. Life's difficulties won't vanish, but they will cease to overwhelm, because your base of happiness and connection will have become strong and secure.

As your fear dissolves, your love will grow; as your love grows, your life will blossom.

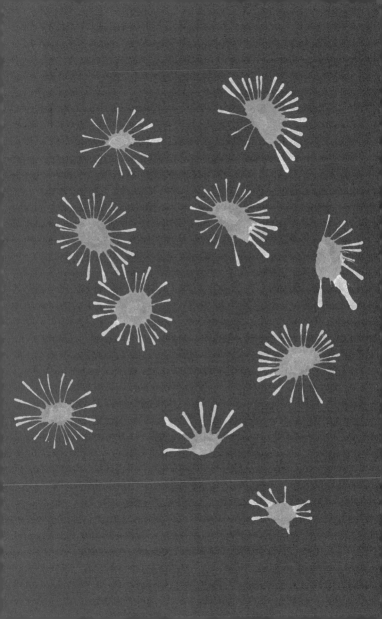

appendix 1
DEEP RELAXATION

When we are not peaceful, when we are in the grip of strong emotions, our bodies can't be peaceful and our breathing can't be peaceful. In times like this, it may be very difficult to practice Ten Breaths. In this case, we can try Deep Relaxation.

This practice takes from ten to fifteen minutes. To do this, find a comfortable position, ideally lying down. Lie down and breathe in and out. Give your body a chance to be there without doing anything; just enjoy the presence of your body. This is total relaxation, the practice of love directed to your body.

You may want to place one or both hands on your belly and feel the rise and fall of your breath:

Breathing in, I am aware of my in-breath.

Breathing out, I am aware of my out-breath.

Begin to pay attention first to your whole body and then to different parts of your body. Go from the top of your head to the soles of your feet. Practice scanning your body with a beam of awareness.

We use the mind to recognize that a certain part of the body is there. Then we send it loving energy and allow that part of the body to relax and release the tension. Ideally, we give each part at least ten in-breaths and out-breaths. The loving energy of smiling can be very helpful. You can send a smile to each part of your body.

Beginning with your face, you can practice like this:

Breathing in, I smile to my face.

Breathing out, I release the tension in my face.

There are hundreds of muscles in your face, and when you're angry or afraid those muscles hold a lot of tension. With relaxation, your face can be completely different after one in-breath and out-breath.

There is often tension in the eyes:

Breathing in, I smile to my eyes.

Breathing out, I release the tension around my eyes.

Become aware of your eyes and smile lovingly to them.

Do the same with your ears:

Breathing in, I smile to my ears.

Breathing out, I release the tension in my ears.

When you come to your shoulders, practice:

Breathing in, I smile to my shoulders.

Breathing out, I release the tension in my shoulders.

Help your shoulders to relax and not be stiff.

When you come to your lungs, embrace your lungs. They work so hard, and we are grateful for them:

Breathing in, I smile to my lungs.

Breathing out, I release the tension in my lungs.

Do the same with your heart:

Breathing in, I smile to my heart.

Breathing out, I release the tension in my heart.

Continue this way through your entire body: arms, hands, liver, intestines, kidneys, hips, legs, and feet.

Each time, use your breath to recognize, embrace, smile, and release tension. Take time, perhaps ten, fifteen, or twenty minutes to scan your body slowly. Smile to each part of your body and help that part of the body to release the tension that is there.

When you come to a part of the body that is ailing, you can stay longer there and spend more time smiling and helping it to release the tension.

With this kind of practice, you can become deeply relaxed and open to life.

appendix 2

REMOVING THE OBJECT

We are seldom upset for the reason we think we are. Linji, the great ninth-century Chinese Zen master and the founder of the lineage of Plum Village, was known for his exhortation to "remove the object." The object is the person or situation we're thinking about, the story in our minds. This practice helps us to remove these objects and come back to the body, where we encounter the real feelings and sensations that manifest as objects in our minds.

In this meditation, we let go of our thinking and focus on the body energy. By following the energy back into our body feelings and sensations, we can find the roots of the tension and the knots that are the drivers of our thinking. We can embrace this tension with love and tenderness, let it unwind and release itself, and we can heal.

The Removing the Object Meditation goes like this:

1 Breathing in, I find my in-breath; breathing out,
  I find my out-breath.

2 Breathing in, I call to mind a charged issue
  (object); breathing out, I open to that issue.

3 Breathing in, I let go of the thinking about the
  issue (object); breathing out, I embrace that energy
  (the feelings and sensations) within my body.

4 Breathing in, I am aware of my body feelings
  and sensations; breathing out, I embrace and
  completely open myself to my body and feelings,
  with kindness and tenderness.

5 Breathing in, I send my in-breath to my body
  and feelings; breathing out, I release the tension
  in my body and feelings.

6 Breathing in, I am aware of my in-breath;
  breathing out, I am aware of my out-breath.

You may want to give each step at least ten breaths. You can spend more time if there is still tension. Sometimes, the energy in the body and feelings can appear to be overwhelming. At other times the energy can seem to be impenetrable. In these situations, we can use a technique called Touch and Rest. In meditation we "touch" the energy of the body feelings and sensations with our breathing for a period of time, for example, for ten or more breaths. Then, we "rest" by opening our eyes to place our attention on something pleasant in the world for another period of time. This provides a safe base for us in the world if the feelings are very strong. It also gives space to the knots inside of us. When we're ready, we can go inside again. In this way, we touch and rest, back and forth, and let the tension unwind.

This kind of deeper meditation—embracing tension areas deep within the body with mindfulness and breathing—can open pathways into the unconscious/ inner child/animal levels of our being. It can be used to invite into our consciousness "the sadness, despair, regrets, and longings that in the past have been difficult for us to touch."* These deeper meditations can often be accompanied by emotional release, including tears, shaking, heating of the body, laughter, and yawning. Held within a loving energy, this kind of emotional release can be very healing.

---

* Thich Nhat Hanh, *Reconciliation: Healing the Inner Child* (Berkeley, CA: Parallax Press, 2010), 51.

appendix 3

THREE TOUCHINGS OF THE EARTH

The Three Touchings of the Earth is a guided meditation to help us directly experience our connections with the Earth and the stream of life: past, present, and future. This meditation is usually practiced lying facedown, but can be done in any position. If you are practicing by yourself, you can record the text and play it back. If your time is limited, it is wonderful just to say the first line of each touching. After a while, you can compose your own version if you like. Here is one of mine, based on my love of natural history.

1 *I touch the Earth, Mother Earth, planet Earth, my home. Touching the Earth, I connect with my ancestors and descendants of my blood, spiritual, and land families.*

Touching the Earth, I connect with my blood ancestors, which include my human ancestors on both my mother's and my father's sides of the family. My blood ancestors also include creatures very different from me: creatures who crawled, and creatures who swam. I am the continuation of the biology of my ancestors, which has been continuously developing on this Earth for over three billion years.

My blood descendants include my own children and all the children of my blood family, including my nephews, nieces, and their families.

My spiritual ancestors include teachers of many religious traditions. They include those—friends, relatives, schoolteachers—who have taught me love, reverence, and happiness. They also include other creatures, like the birds, who throw back their heads in song and show us how to sing.

My spiritual descendants include all those whom I touch with love and understanding.

My land ancestors include all creatures of this land—people, animals, plants, and minerals—who have come before me, and who support my life. My land descendants include all creatures of this land who are touched by my actions and carry them on into the future.

All ancestors and descendants—we are all part of a constantly moving stream of life.

2   *I touch the Earth, Mother Earth, planet Earth, my home. Touching the Earth, I connect with the Earth and all beings who are present, at this moment, in this world, with me.*

The Earth's minerals are knit into my flesh and my bones. The air entering my chest contains life-giving oxygen made by the plants. In each cell of my body, I carry the salty liquid of my ancestral oceans. The sun's energy powers my breathing, my heart, and my thoughts.

In my food, I see the flesh and bodies of many other creatures. I see how the sustenance of my life and the gathering of my possessions affects the lives of other people, animals, plants, and minerals. I am the frog swimming in the pond, and I am also the snake that seeks to eat the frog to nourish itself. I can see that I am part of the web of life.

In this body, I can also see the presence of great time and great care. I see my connections with all beings, and I see their connections with me.

3   *I touch the Earth, Mother Earth, planet Earth,*
    my home. Touching the Earth, I let go of the idea
    that my life is this body and I let go of the idea that
    I have a life span that is confined to this particular
    period of time.

I can see my life in the past, in the present, and in the future. I can see my life before my body manifested and after my body dissolves. I can see that I am part of a constantly moving stream—of blood, spiritual, and land ancestors—that for billions of years has been flowing into the present and flows on into the future.

My life is supported by and always in relationship with the Earth, the cosmos, and countless other beings. I can see that my body is constantly dissolving, and reemerging, like my actions, into many other forms.

I can go beyond the idea that I am a self, separated in time and space from other people and other forms of life and the rest of the world. We are all waves on the ocean, each made of the same ancestral water, connected and interdependent.

We are each a splendid thread in the tapestry of the world, woven here, together, on our big spinning ball of a planet, circling around the Sun, our star. This is real.

ACKNOWLEDGMENTS

I give thanks to our countless blood, spiritual, and land ancestors. I have felt their love and wisdom flowing through my body and into this book.

In our time, very special thanks to Caleb Cushing for agitating to "write this up," and for his steady support, some of the best phrases, and big heart. It was Caleb who once said, astonished, "Are you sure this practice is legal?"

Thanks to Terry Helbick-White and Rick Hanson for opening my eyes to rooting happiness in neural pathways. Thanks to Natascha Bruckner for printing the earliest version in *The Mindfulness Bell*. Thanks to Travis Masch, Rachel Neumann, and Terry Barber of Parallax Press for convincing me to write the book, and to the whole staff there. Thanks to editor Tai Moses, artist Jason DeAntonis, and designer Elaine Chow. Thanks to great volunteer editors, Connie Jacowitz and Sharon Moy.

Thanks to those who have cheered me on, helped test the practice, and shared their stories, including Betty, Lyn, Chau, Ilana, Denise, Jo-Ann, Stiles, Diana, Ruby, Brandy, Peter, Lennis, Sarah, Brigitte, David, Miriam, Augusta, the Buckeye Sangha, the Potluck Sangha, and so many others.

May our efforts bring happiness to all beings, beginning with ourselves.

JIJYUZANMAI

Abandoning myself to breathing out
And letting breathing in naturally fill me
All that is left is an empty zafu
Under a vast sky,
The weight of a flame.

—KEIZAN ZENJI, 1268–1325

Translated by Dai-En Benage Roshi
with thanks to Mitchell Ratner

Parallax Press, a nonprofit organization,
publishes books on engaged Buddhism
and the practice of mindfulness by
Thich Nhat Hanh and other authors.
For a copy of the free catalog, please contact:

Parallax Press
P.O. Box 7355
Berkeley, CA 94707
Tel: (510) 525-0101
www.parallax.org

Monastics and laypeople practice the art of mindful
living in the tradition of Thich Nhat Hanh at retreat
communities worldwide. To reach any of these communities,
or for information about individuals and families joining
for a practice period, please contact:

Plum Village
13 Martineau
33580 Dieulivol, France
www.plumvillage.org

Magnolia Grove Monastery
123 Towles Rd.
Batesville, MS 38606
www.magnoliagrovemonastery.org

Blue Cliff Monastery
3 Mindfulness Road
Pine Bush, NY 12566
www.bluecliffmonastery.org

Deer Park Monastery
2499 Melru Lane
Escondido, CA 92026
www.deerparkmonastery.org

The Mindfulness Bell, a journal of the art of mindful living in
the tradition of Thich Nhat Hanh, is published three times
a year by Plum Village. To subscribe or to see the worldwide
directory of Sanghas, visit www.mindfulnessbell.org